Classifying Organisms

by Wade Lind

PEARSON
Scott
Foresman

Why do we classify?

Lewis and Clark's Mission of Discovery

From 1804 to 1806, Meriwether Lewis and William Clark led a team across North America. Along the way, they saw many new plants and animals. Lewis and Clark described each organism carefully. They also gathered many samples. Later, scientists observed and compared the samples.

Scientists then used what they learned to classify organisms. To **classify** is to put things into groups. Some plants and animals did not fit into any group. New groups needed to be made for these organisms.

Reasons to Classify

A classification system gives each organism its own special name. This helps scientists know exactly what organism another scientist is talking about.

Scientists can also learn things about an organism just by knowing how it is classified. For example, something classified as a plant most likely needs light to live.

Classification Systems

A classification system lists organisms in a series of groups. The system we use today has been used for many years. Scientists are always changing the system to make it better. At one time, plants and animals were the only forms of life known. So scientists divided all life into the plant and animal kingdoms. A **kingdom** is the largest and most general group in the classification system. A system often used today has six kingdoms.

A kingdom is divided into a smaller group called a **phylum.** This group is divided into smaller and smaller groups. They are the **class,** order, family, genus, and the smallest group, the **species.**

The bison is a member of the animal kingdom.

Six Kingdoms of Living Things

Archaebacteria

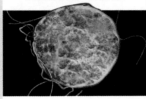

Archaebacteria live as single cells. Many do not need oxygen or sunlight to live.

Eubacteria

Eubacteria are single cells. They have cell parts that archaebacteria do not have.

Protists

Most protists are single cells, but some have many cells. Algae are protists.

Fungi

Mushrooms and molds are fungi. Fungi can be made of one or many cells.

Plants

Plants have many cells. They make their own sugar for food.

Animals

Animals have many cells. They get their food by eating other organisms.

How do we classify vertebrates?

Class: Fish

Clownfish

Characteristics of Animals

Animals are different from other kinds of organisms in many ways. Animals are made of more than one cell. Animals need to eat other organisms for energy, because they cannot make their own food. They can also move on their own for at least part of their lives.

Vertebrate Animals

The animal kingdom is divided into more than thirty phyla. One phylum contains a subphylum of animals with backbones. These animals are called **vertebrates.** Mammals, birds, reptiles, amphibians, and fish are the five classes of vertebrates.

Class: Amphibians

Golden-Lined Frog

Mammals

Most mammals have hair or fur. They breathe air through lungs. Mothers make milk for their babies. Mammals go through a pattern of birth, growth, reproduction, and death. This is called a life cycle. Mammal babies usually look like their parents when they are born.

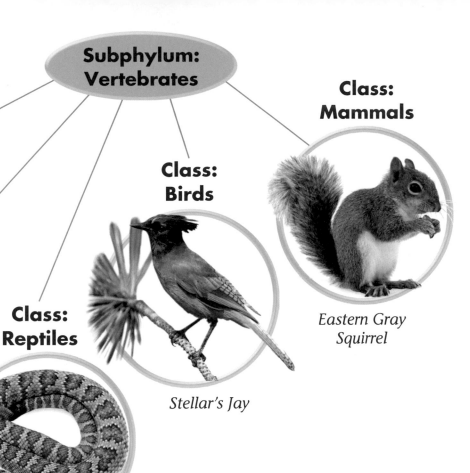

Subphylum: Vertebrates

Class: Mammals

Class: Birds

Class: Reptiles

Eastern Gray Squirrel

Stellar's Jay

Western Diamondback Rattlesnake

Reptiles

Reptiles are like mammals in many ways. They have lungs, stomachs, eyes, noses, and mouths. But they do not look like mammals. They have tough skin, and scales instead of fur or hair.

Reptiles are cold-blooded, meaning their temperature changes with the air or water around them. If the air is cold, a reptile will become cold. Their body temperature changes all the time. Mammals are warm-blooded. Their body temperature is the same almost all the time.

Life Cycle of Reptiles

Another difference between reptiles and mammals is the way they are born. Unlike mammals, reptiles lay eggs. Babies are ready to live on their own when they are hatched. They don't need their parents' help to find food.

Birds

Birds are like mammals in some ways. They have many similar organs, and they are warm-blooded.

There is one thing that makes birds different from all other animals. Can you guess what it is? It is not their ability to fly. Not all birds can fly, but insects and bats can. What makes birds different from all other animals is that they have feathers.

Life Cycle of Birds

The life cycle of birds is much like that of reptiles. Both hatch from eggs. But baby birds must be fed by their parents. Reptiles can find their own food as soon as they are hatched.

Amphibians

Amphibians include frogs, toads, and salamanders. Amphibians are cold-blooded, like reptiles. They are different in many ways, though. Amphibians have soft, moist skin, while reptiles have hard scales.

Life Cycle of Amphibians

Most vertebrates are born looking like their parents. The way they look stays the same for their whole lives. But amphibians go through big changes as they grow up. For example, a frog hatches from its egg as a tadpole. The tadpole has a tail, but no legs. It gets oxygen through gills. But when it grows up, it turns into a frog. Frogs have legs, but no tails. They breathe air through lungs.

Fish

There are some mammals and reptiles that live in water. But every member of the fish class spends its entire life in the water. They get oxygen through gills. Most fish have scales just as reptiles do. The life cycle of a fish is most like a reptile's life cycle.

1 An egg is the first step of the life cycle. The salamander grows in the egg.

2 The salamander hatches as a larva.

5 Most fully grown salamanders do not have gills. They have lungs.

4 The salamander grows and develops.

3 The larva gets oxygen through gills that look like feathers on its head.

11

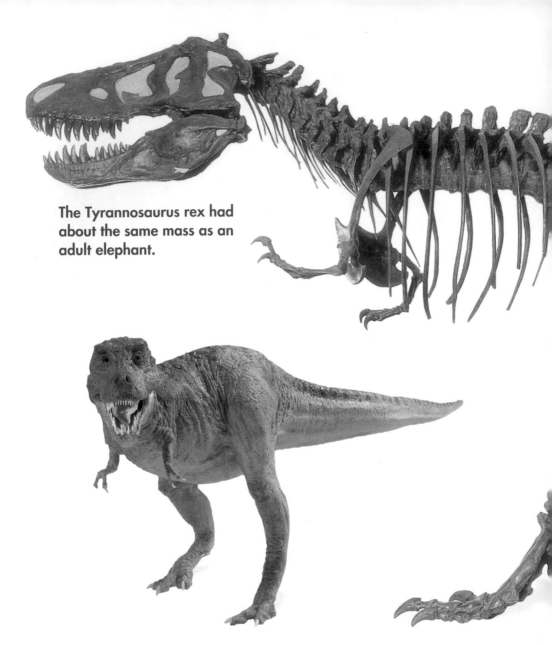

The Tyrannosaurus rex had about the same mass as an adult elephant.

Discovery of Dinosaur Fossils

In the early 1800s, scientists began classifying the fossils of ancient animal bones. They compared the fossils to the bones of living animals. Scientists found that the ancient animals were very similar to modern lizards, but many of them were huge. They named the fossil animals *dinosaurs,* which means "terrible lizards."

Comparing Dinosaurs to Today's Animals

Dinosaurs were like modern lizards in many ways. They had scales and backbones. Many walked on four legs.

There are differences between dinosaurs and lizards however. Dinosaurs' legs went almost straight down from their bodies. Lizards' legs stick out from their sides. Some dinosaurs had feathers and wishbones, as birds have. Also, the heart of some dinosaurs was much like a bird's or a mammal's heart.

How do we classify invertebrates?

Animals Without Backbones

When we think of animals, we often think of vertebrates. But most of the animals on Earth do not have backbones. Animals without backbones are **invertebrates.**

Some invertebrates are too small to be seen with just the eye. The largest one, the giant squid, can stretch the width of a basketball court! Mollusks, worms, corals, and arthropods are all types of invertebrates.

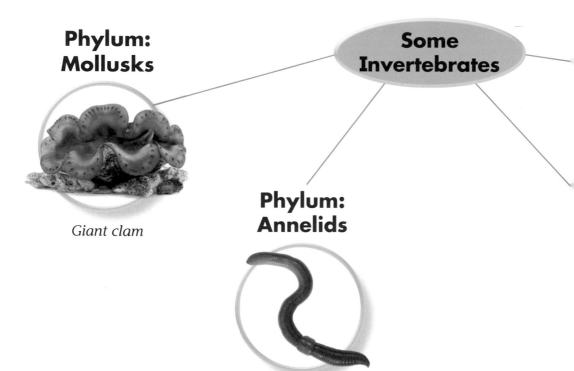

Phylum: Mollusks

Giant clam

Some Invertebrates

Phylum: Annelids

Earthworm

Mollusks

A mollusk is a kind of invertebrate that has a soft body. Some mollusks, such as clams and snails, have hard shells. Squids and slugs are also mollusks. Some mollusks get oxygen by using gills. Others take it in through their skin.

Worms

There are many different kinds of worms. Flatworms are very thin and flat. Roundworms can live on land or in water. The earthworm is just one kind of segmented worm. Some worms cannot be seen without a microscope. Others can be several meters long.

This mollusk is called a lettuce sea slug. Can you guess how it got its name?

Phylum: Arthropods

Moth

Phylum: Cnidarians

Jellyfish

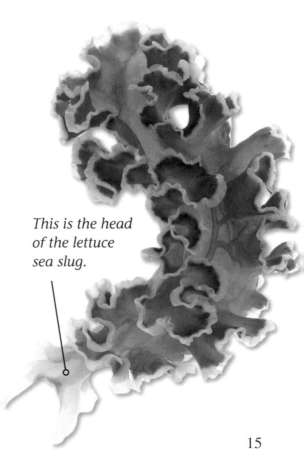

This is the head of the lettuce sea slug.

15

Jellyfish Life Cycle

The phylum Cnidaria includes invertebrates such as jellyfish and coral. The life cycle of a jellyfish is very different from the life cycles of vertebrates.

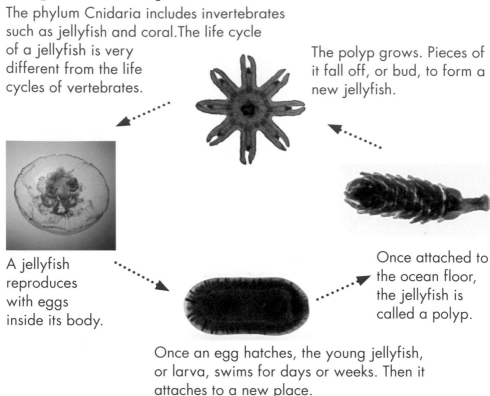

The polyp grows. Pieces of it fall off, or bud, to form a new jellyfish.

A jellyfish reproduces with eggs inside its body.

Once attached to the ocean floor, the jellyfish is called a polyp.

Once an egg hatches, the young jellyfish, or larva, swims for days or weeks. Then it attaches to a new place.

Arthropods

Arthropods include insects, lobsters, and spiders. The word *arthropod* means "jointed feet." Some arthropods get oxygen through gills. Others have special tubes that carry air through their bodies. They all have hard outer coverings and bodies that are divided into several parts. The arthropod phylum has more animals in it than any other in the animal kingdom.

Complete Metamorphosis

Some arthropods, such as butterflies, go through big changes during their life cycles. This kind of life cycle is called complete metamorphosis. Other arthropods, such as grasshoppers, hatch from eggs looking like adults. Their life cycle is called incomplete metamorphosis.

An egg is the first stage of a life cycle with complete metamorphosis.

The second stage is a larva that does not look like an adult. A butterfly larva is a caterpillar. Another arthropod larva may be a maggot or grub.

After it has grown, a larva goes through a pupa stage. A butterfly pupa is a chrysalis.

After the pupa stage, the butterfly is changed into the adult form.

Identifying Organisms

A useful tool for identifying an organism is a dichotomous (deye-KOT-uh-muhs) key. This tool uses a set of questions to help identify living things in a certain classification. Look at the key on the next page. Use it to identify the animal below. The first question asks if the animal has jointed legs. It does, so we can follow the "yes" arrow to learn that the animal is an arthropod.

The second question asks how many legs the animal has. We can see that the animal has six legs. By following the arrow next to the number six, we learn that the animal is an insect. The next question asks if the animal has a long neck. By answering "yes," we learn that the animal is a giraffe weevil.

Dichotomous Key

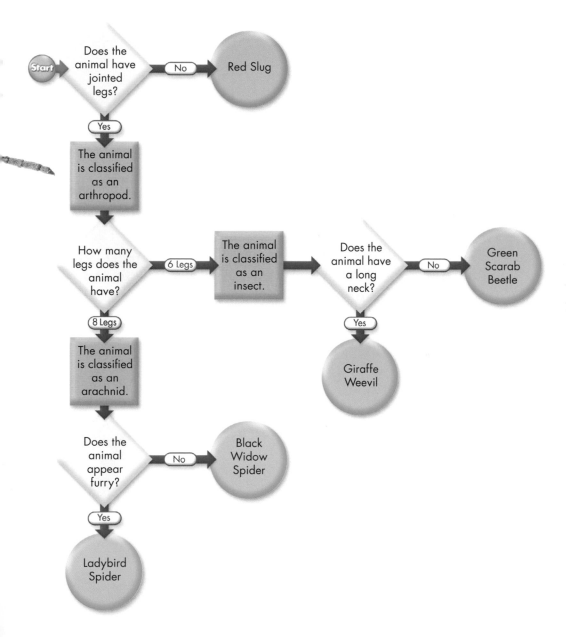

Does the animal have jointed legs? — No → Red Slug

Yes → The animal is classified as an arthropod.

How many legs does the animal have? — 6 Legs → The animal is classified as an insect. → Does the animal have a long neck? — No → Green Scarab Beetle

Yes → Giraffe Weevil

8 Legs → The animal is classified as an arachnid. → Does the animal appear furry? — No → Black Widow Spider

Yes → Ladybird Spider

How are other organisms classified?

Qualities of Plants

Organisms in the plant kingdom have many cells, just as animals do. But, unlike animals, plants make their own food from sunlight, water, and carbon dioxide. Plants have special parts, such as roots and leaves.

Mosses

Mosses are groups of tiny plants that grow together. They do not have flowers or seeds. Mosses grow on trees or in shallow water.

Cushion moss

Fiddlehead fern

Ferns

Ferns have leaves that look like feathers. Like mosses, they do not have seeds or flowers. Both use spores to reproduce. Unlike mosses, ferns are vascular plants. This means they have tubes running through them to carry food and water to all their parts. These plants can grow larger than nonvascular plants.

Conifers

The conifer phylum includes pine and spruce trees. Conifers are vascular plants. They reproduce using cones and seeds. The needles of conifers are really special leaves.

Flowering Plants

These vascular plants use colorful flowers to make seeds and reproduce. Mosses, ferns, and conifers do not have flowers.

Neither Plant Nor Animal

Many organisms are neither plants nor animals. Some of them can move on their own like animals, but they make their own food like plants. Some of these life forms may be just a single cell. Some are groups of single cells that can live on their own, but are helped by living together. Some tiny organisms cause disease. But most are harmless. Some are even helpful.

Even though these organisms are not plants or animals, they have similar needs. They need food and water, and they need to get rid of waste. Some need gases such as carbon dioxide or oxygen.

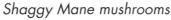
Shaggy Mane mushrooms

Fungi Kingdom
Fungi are not plants, because they cannot make their own food. Instead, they absorb food from the material they grow on. Mushrooms are fungi.

Diatom

Protist Kingdom
Most protists are single cells. Some live in colonies. Protists such as algae are food for many animals. Some protists even live inside an animal's digestive system and help it digest its food.

Debates in Classifying

Not everyone agrees about how to classify life. Some people think there should be only four or five kingdoms. Sometimes when a new organism is found, scientists disagree over what group it belongs to. The classification system will probably keep changing as new life is discovered.

Eubacteria

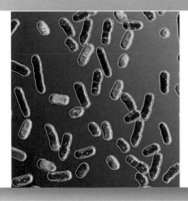

Eubacteria Kingdom
Eubacteria are single cells. They have many different shapes. Some look like spheres, rods, or even spirals.

Archaebacteria

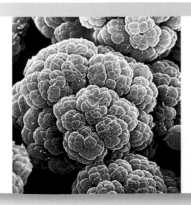

Archaebacteria Kingdom
These are single-celled organisms that can survive in places that would kill other life forms. They can live in very salty water, or in hot acid springs.

Glossary

class   the level of classification below phylum

classify   to put things into groups

invertebrate   an animal without a backbone

kingdom   the most general group in the system for classifying living things

phylum   the level below kingdom in the system for classifying living things

species   the smallest group in the system for classifying living things

vertebrate   an animal with a backbone